SUCCESSFUL, SENSIBLE BOOK MARKETING TIPS

Lorraine M. Harris

Copyright © 2018 Lorraine M. Harris

ISBN-13-9781719569910

ISBN-10-1719569916

All rights reserved. No one will reproduce any part of this book, stored in a retrieval system or transmitted in any form or by any means without prior written permission of the author. The exception is if a reviewer wants to quote brief passages in a review for printing in a magazine, newspaper, or journal.

Printed in the United States.

DEDICATION

To my loving and supportive husband, Lamont and my daughters, Nicole and Natalie Harris Lenz and husband, Richard Scott Lenz. They are always supportive and encouraging.

ACKNOWLEDGEMENTS

My Lord and Savior is why I write and to Him I owe my talents and gifts. To keep me motivated, I rely on my favorite verse, Philippians 4:13, *"I know that I can do all things through him who strengthens me."*

Everyone needs friends and confidantes to give you honest critique along with encouragement. I am fortunate to have The Write Corner members who are amazing, award-winning published female authors.

My daughter, Natalie is my biggest critic. A special thanks to her for providing me with candid feedback.

Inspiration for this book came from my experience after having my first book published. I had no idea how to market, promote, and sell my book and took notes on what worked and what didn't work. I shared the information with various writing groups and with encouragement from the Tampa Florida Writers Association members, I wrote, *Marketing Tips for Self-Published Authors.*

After ten years of writing and publishing, I decided to update my first book by providing detailed information on what has worked successfully for me.
Although I want my books to be error free that doesn't

always happen. I take full responsibility for all mistakes and hope they don't interfere with those using the information in this book.

When I wrote this book, the contents reflected my views acquired through my experiences. At the time of publication, the sources mentioned were reliable, but since then, websites and prices may have changed.

TABLE OF CONTENTS

INTRODUCTION

CHAPTER 1

CHAPTER 2

CHAPTER 3

CHAPTER 4

CHAPTER 5

CHAPTER 6

CHAPTER 7

CHAPTER 8

CHAPTER 9

CHAPTER 10

CHAPTER 11

CHAPTER 12

CHAPTER 13

CHAPTER 14

CHAPTER 15

CHAPTER 16

CHAPTER 17

CHAPTER 18

CHAPTER 19

CHAPTER 20

CHAPTER 21

CHAPTER 22

CHAPTER 23

CHAPTER 24

CHAPTER 25

CHAPTER 26

CHAPTER 27

CHAPTER 28

CHAPTER 29

CHAPTER 30

CHAPTER 31

CHAPTER 32

CHAPTER 33

CHAPTER 34

CHAPTER 35

CHAPTER 36

CHAPTER 37

RESOURCES

INTRODUCTION

I became a published author over ten years ago and couldn't have predicted the reality of what that meant. If people were to buy my books, I had the responsibility for marketing, promoting, and selling my books.

My journey of selling books has been hard, but I've learned some invaluable lessons. My hope in writing this book is to share my experience by helping other authors find success in selling their books. Before I share the details of my success, let me start from the beginning.

Sunday Golf, my first published book, was my dream come true. My desire to become an author ended when my fourth-grade teacher asked me what I wanted to be when I grow up. My response was, "I want to be an author."

Frowning, my teacher said, "You need to consider another career because authors don't make money."

Discouraged, I took her advice and found a career in the federal government. After retirement, I wrote my first novel. After submitting it to many publishers, I received the most unbelievable surprise. One publisher accepted my book and would publish it.

My excitement of having my dream come true soon diminished when the publisher asked for my marketing plan. "A what?" was my response.

I wasn't prepared for the publisher's explanation. "You need to develop a plan about how you will market, promote, and sell your book."

I wanted to say, "I thought that was the publisher's job," but I didn't.

To make sure, I didn't miss anything else, I reviewed my contract, again. Thank goodness, there wasn't any more surprises, but I did read the section that stated, "The author has to prepare a detailed marketing plan." How did I miss that?

Stunned, I didn't know what to do or where to start in developing a marketing plan. To add insult to injury, my loving husband kept reminding me about the boxes of books I had bought and were taking up space in the garage.

He kept saying, "No one knows who you are and your contract states that selling your book is your responsibility.

I understood what to do, but that didn't make it any easier. All I wanted was to start writing my next book, not sell books.

I'm embarrassed to admit it, but my husband's constant, irritating reminders, motivated me to do something. To make matters worse, he asked, "Can I see your marketing plan?"

"No," I said with a forced smile. "I'm still working on it."

In reality, I hadn't started it. Every time I tried working on my plan, it was overwhelming. I wasn't prepared to do so many varied duties related to marketing, promoting, and selling a book. Below are just a few of those jobs.

- Book agent
- Publicist
- Promoter
- Salesperson
- Presenter

Like most authors, I resisted the idea of selling my book. However, if I didn't do it, my books weren't going to sell themselves. After buying and borrowing books, I learned the following on the subject.

- ➢ Most of the information didn't say what produced the best results.

- ➢ Marketing is expensive.

- ➢ Many of the strategies on marketing, promoting, and selling books spoke in generalities but they didn't give the nuts and bolts of how to do them.

Many of the books had a common thread about why people buy books and that information was useful and eye-opening. Below is what I learned about people who buy books.

- ➢ People borrow books from the library, friends, neighbors, and relatives, but they seldom buy books.

- ➢ Genre readers are people who buy books in a particular area such as fiction, romance, mystery, sci-fi, or non-fiction.

- ➢ Avid readers read two to three books a week. They don't find it cost-effective to buy new books, so they go to libraries, flea markets, used-book stores, and yard sales.

- Authors have people who read their books and they become fans. These individuals talk about the author and recommend people to buy their books.

After all these years, I still haven't found many helpful books on marketing for self-published authors. One of my biggest challenges is the cost of marketing. Being retired and on a fixed income, I had to find free or low-cost strategies.

I did read three books on the subject I found relevant and helpful.

- 1001 Ways to Market Your Books, John Kremer (Open Horizons 2009)

- Guerrilla Publicity, Jay Conrad Levinson, Rick Frishman, and Jill Lublin (Adams Media Corporation)

- How to Write, Print and Sell Your Book, Dan Poynter (ParaPublishing, 2009)

Based on these books, I developed a marketing plan, doing the easiest and cost-effective strategies. I made my husband happy, but he didn't celebrate until I began selling books.

At last, I developed a plan, kept it as simple as possible. and included the following strategies.

- Identify bookstores and other venues where I could have book signings.

- Create a website.

- Contact newspapers and magazines where I could have interviews.

- Tell relatives, friends, and neighbors about my published book.

I included times for accomplishing each item and tracked what gave me the most bang for my dollar. All others I dismissed.

****

Since the release of my first book, the publishing industry changed. Technology has made marketing different because of how people learn about books and how they buy them. Many individuals turn to the following social media sites when it comes to books.

- Twitter

- Pinterest

- Facebook

- Instagram

****

Since I'm retired, and on a fixed budget, I wrote this book similar to my first one titled, *Marketing Tips for Self-Published Authors*. I tried to make the book's format easy to read as well as considering the following items.

- ➢ Useful
- ➢ Effortless
- ➢ Cheap or free
- ➢ Timesaving

This book is not all-inclusive. You must understand that what works for me, may or may not work for other authors. Some of these ideas may seem a little brazen while others may not seem that creative.

Some of the ideas from my first book are still worth repeating, and I've included them in this book. All information was current when I wrote the book.

My goal is to help authors use their imaginative juices to market, promote, and sell books. In time, many of your ideas will probably be bolder than mine.

This book should be viewed as a working document. Below are things you need to consider if you want success.

- Learn patience.
- Be persistent.
- Make time to market, promote, and sell your book.
- Become confident.
- Do one strategy at once.

CHAPTER 1
MARKETING PLAN

If you've written or finished your novel, it's important that every author needs a marketing plan. You don't have to make it elaborate.

Why have a plan? What will it do for an author? My experience taught me the following about having a plan.

- Stay focused.

- Track progress.

- Know what works.

- Learn to be flexible, making changes when needed.

My suggestion is to keep your plan simple. Below is an easy outline of a marketing plan that might help you get started.

MARKETING PLAN SAMPLE

INTRODUCTION—Provide a summary of your book; current market conditions; summarize budgets; identify readers; goals and objectives; and marketing strategies.

CHAPTER 1—Be specific as to who would be interested in buying your book. Below are examples.

- ➢ Children's book—teachers, moms, librarians, etc.

- ➢ Romance novels—single and married women.

CHAPTER 2—Explain your book's goal.

CHAPTER 3—Provide at a minimum, the following in your marketing plan:

- ➢ **Objectives**—Steps to achieve your goal such as setting up events to promote your book; obtain reviews of your book; online resources for promoting your book and finding non-retail opportunities to sell your book.

- ➢ **Plans and Actions**—Plans to get your objectives moving such as setting up one book signing, a month; obtaining two interviews in the first quarter; and becoming a guest speaker at one book club, library, etc. in the second quarter.

CHAPTER 4—Create a reasonable timeline and budget for marketing your book. The amount of money you have to spend will determine what and how much you can do. Listed below are monetary expenses you might expect.

- Giving away books.

- Marketing materials such as posters, flyers, and business cards.

- Mailing books.

Helpful Marketing Plan Tips:

- Learn to be flexible, making changes when needed.

- Determine the cost of each strategy.

- Think about what you're going to do and how much time you're going to spend on marketing, promoting, and selling your book.

CHAPTER 2
START A CONTACT LIST

To me, one of the most important items an author needs is a contact list. If you don't have one, it's never too late to start one.

Part of your success is reaching your audience. To do so, you must find people to buy your books.

You say you don't know where to start. It's easier than you might think. Everyone has physical and email addresses of relatives and friends. Start to create your list from the following sources.

- Personal telephone and address books.
- Christmas card list.
- High school yearbooks.
- College alumni yearbooks.

Go through these books and make a list of the people you know, noting their name, home, and email addresses.

Helpful Contact List Tips:

- ➤ To maintain and track your list, do what's comfortable. Use Word, Excel or other computer programs.

- ➤ If not computer literate, use a three-ring notebook.

CHAPTER 3
CONTACT LIST FROM DIRECTORIES

You have a list started. Now comes the hard work. Finding ways to add names to the list. You can do that by gathering names of people you don't know from an array of directories. Below are examples of directories you can use.

<u>NEIGHORHOOD DIRECTORY</u>—Check to see if your neighborhood has a directory of the residents. If they have one, get it. Below is how you might use it.

- ✓ Increase your list by including the neighbor's home and email addresses.

Helpful Neighborhood Directory Tip:

- ➢ Create a neighborhood directory if one doesn't exist, explain the need for having it. You might say that it provides an opportunity for residents to know their neighbors and useful during emergencies.

CHURCH DIRECTORY—If you go to church, check to see if they have a membership directory, get a copy, and use it in several ways.

- ✓ Add church members' home and email addresses to your current contact list.

Helpful Church Directory Tips:

- ➤ When you attend church, sit in the same row or general area. Before the service begins, introduce yourself to people sitting near you and engage them in conversation. Weeks later and after you get to know the individuals, give the person a business card, get one from them and begin to build your own church directory.

- ➤ Depending on the size of the congregation, volunteer to make a church directory.

TELEPHONE DIRECTORY—Everyone receives a local telephone directory and you can use it in several ways.

- ✓ Start with the first name in the directory and add the name and home address.

ORGANIZATION/CLUB DIRCTORY—If you belong to an organization or club such as a Book Club, Rotary Club or Lion's Club, ask for a copy of the membership directory.

Helpful Organization/Club Directory Tips:

- ➢ If you don't belong to any organization or club, ask members for a copy of their membership directory. Tell the person why you want it and if you can use their name when sending out announcements regarding your book signing events.

- ➢ Be aware, you will spend money on the cost of paper or postcards, and stamps.

- ➢ Send a thank you note to the person who gave you a list of members.

FAMILY REUNION LIST—If your family has a family reunion, talk to the host for a copy of the relatives home and email addresses.

CLASS REUNION DIRECTORY—When you attend a class reunion, make sure you receive a copy of the Class Reunion Directory. If one doesn't exist, ask the class reunion committee if you can have a copy of the list of class members' home and email addresses.

Helpful Tip:

➤ If a Class Reunion Directory doesn't exist, you might want to volunteer to make one for the next reunion.

CHAPTER 4
EMAIL CONTACT LIST

With technology, I realized that my contact list was turning into an email contact list. If you aren't on the Internet, it's a must to sign up for social media sites.

- ✓ Facebook
- ✓ Twitter
- ✓ Instagram
- ✓ Pinterest

Once you create an account, you can gather email addresses, and a source for you to add names to your email contact list.

Helpful Email Contact List Tips:

Once you obtain email addresses from various social media, you can do the following to spread the word about your book and gain followers that can turn into potential buyers for your book.

- Send out tweets and Facebook posts before and after a book event.

- Post pictures on Facebook, Instagram, and Pinterest before and after a book event.

- Have another person send a tweet or post on Facebook, your book or book event information.

CHAPTER 5
FACEBOOK FAN PAGE

FACEBOOK FAN PAGE— Facebook is a free social media and social networking website. For authors, it's good to have a personal page as well as a Facebook Fan Page. Once you sign up you can use it to do a large number of activities.

- ✓ Create a profile.

- ✓ Upload photos.

- ✓ Upload videos.

- ✓ Send messages.

- ✓ Keep in touch with family, friends, authors and most importantly your readers.

This is an amazing way to promote yourself as an author; build awareness of who you are, and to advertise. Below are instructions for creating a Facebook Fan Page.

1. Sign up for Facebook. If you already have an account, log in.

2. Click on the settings, near the top right-hand corner of the page.

    ✓ Click on "Advertising."

    ✓ Look under Step 1: Build Your Facebook Page.

    ✓ Click on "Create a Page."

3. Click on the type of page you want to create. There are six categories—select "Artist" and author should appear.

4. Click on "Get Started."

5. Upload a profile picture.

6. Complete the About Section.

7. Decide whether you want to enable ads—this will cost and it can be expensive with little or no results.

Helpful Facebook Fan Page Tips:

➢ Post often, authors need to keep their page current.

➢ Post pictures of all author events, not only book activities. Other pictures let readers know more about authors. For example, you ran in the Relay for Life 5K to raise money for cancer.

CHAPTER 6
AMAZON AUTHOR PAGE

AMAZON AUTHOR CENTRAL—Amazon Author Central is a free service provided by Amazon. It enables authors to reach more readers, promote books, and help people learn about you.

Most authors have their books on Amazon, yet they don't always setup an account on Amazon Author Central. Any author with a book listed on Amazon is eligible to sign up for Amazon Author Central.

Author Central is a platform that allows authors to setup an Author Page on Amazon. The page is where people can learn more about you and buy all your books, find your website, or social media. You can do the following on the Author Page.

- ✓ Add editorial reviews.
- ✓ Track book sales.
- ✓ Read and respond to reviews.

- ✓ Chat with readers.

- ✓ Fix issues with your book listing.

- ✓ Allows people to keep track of things such as your blog, book releases, etc.

Below are instructions for creating an Amazon Author Page.

1. Go to https://authorcentral.amazon.com/ and click **Join Now**.

2. Sign in with your regular Amazon username and password.

3. Select new customer if you don't have an Amazon account.

4. Read the Terms and Conditions then click **Accept**.

5. Enter the name of your books and the author's name used to write your book.

6. Must select a book because that's how your account is created.

Helpful Amazon Author Page Tips:

- ➢ Your book must be sold on Amazon.

- Use your ISBN to find your book.

- Amazon will send you a confirmation email to finish creating your account.

- While waiting for verification, you can start adding information such as your bio, profile, and pictures.

CHAPTER 7
MARKETING EVENTS

Before an author has a book signing event, do everything to market it. Depending on the type of event, do everything to entice people to attend.

Don't just tell people about the location, date, and time of the event, explain why they should come. Below are items you might use.

- ✓ Give a good description of the event.

- ✓ Describe the benefits for why a person should attend the event such as free prizes, food, celebrity appearance, and workshops.

- ✓ Post an image of the event on items such as book marks, flyers, and social media.

- ✓ Gather positive comments from people that attended the event last year and include them on items such as bookmarks, flyers, and social media.

- ✓ Talk about the workshops and speakers appearing at the event.
- ✓ Make sure all information talks about how many authors will participate in the event.

- ✓ Make a list of some of the well-known authors participating at the event and include them on items such as book marks, flyers, and social media.

Below are other ways of telling people about your event.

- ✓ Send a letter or email blast to everyone on the author's contact list, telling them about the event, giving as much information as possible.

- ✓ Ask organization or club members if you can use their name. Send a letter, postcard, or email to the names given to you.

    In the first paragraph, include the member's name. Explain why they're receiving correspondence from you. Be creative with your letter. Below is an example of what you might say.

Dear Mr. Smith,

Hi, my name is Lorraine M. Harris, and I'm a friend of Larry Jones who is the President of the Lion's Club. I hope you don't mind, but I'm a published author and I'm trying to let people know about my newly released book.

My book title is "Amy's Autumn Splendor" and below is the book's synopsis, cost, places to buy it.

You get the idea.

Helpful Marketing Event Tips:

➢ Budget for the cost of items such as paper, envelopes, postcards, and stamps.

CHAPTER 8
NON-TRADITIONAL BOOK SIGNINGS

When it comes to having a book signing, look beyond the traditional book signings held in bookstores, book expos, and festivals. Think out-of-the box. Authors can have book signings almost anywhere. Just ask if you can have one.

Authors should consider a variety of nontraditional book signing opportunities.

Family Reunions—Lots of people have family reunions. You might not attend them but you might miss an opportunity for telling relatives you know and don't know that you're a published author. Do the following when planning to attend a family reunion.

- ✓ Ask the host or family reunion coordinator if you can have a book signing. If you can't, ask if you can talk to family members about your journey as an author and perhaps write the family story.

- ✓ Be prepared to sell your books even if you can't have a book signing.

- ✓ Obtain names, email and home addresses that you can add to your contact list.

Class Reunions—When you receive an invitation to attend your high school or college reunion, plan to attend. Do the following ideas.

- ✓ Contact the class reunion coordinator or committee and ask if you can have a book signing.

- ✓ Bring books with you and be prepared to sell books even if you can't have a book signing.

- ✓ Ask if you can donate a door prize. Put together a basket that includes a copy of your books.

- ✓ Obtain a copy of the class reunion directory that will have email and home addresses. Another way you can build your contact list.

- ✓ Pass out your business card.

Helpful Class Reunion Tip:

- ➤ At the reunion, socialize with not only familiar class members but get to know the ones you didn't know.

Church Events—If you attend church, find out if they have a book club.

- ✓ Identify the church you want to contact.

- ✓ Call the church and explain that you're an author. Ask if they have a book club, ask for the point-of-contact, and call the person about having a book signing.

Helpful Church Tip:

- ➤ Even if you don't attend a church, it shouldn't stop you from contacting churches, obtaining information about book clubs.

Cruises—If you're going on a cruise, contact the Entertainment Cruise Director.

- ✓ Explain that you're an author and ask if you can have a book signing.

Restaurants—If you mentioned a particular restaurant in your book, call the manager.

- ✓ Explain that you're an author, give the manager a book, and ask if you can have a book signing.

- ✓ Ask if you can put a book display on the counter or somewhere else in the restaurant if you can't have a book signing.

Book Signing Party—Sponsor your own book signing party. Think of it like any other merchandise party where you're selling a product. Do the following for the party.

- ✓ Decide where to have the party and the cost for having it.

- ✓ Identify who to invite.

- ✓ Send out invitations, explaining that it's a book signing. Make sure you tell them that they can buy your book and the cost.

- ✓ Ask people to let you know if they'll attend. If someone says they can't attend, add another person. You can also tell the people who can't attend how they can buy your book.

Helpful Book Party Tips:

- ➢ Keep your party small if having it in your home. Easier to manage and you can track who buys your book.

- ➢ Ask people you invite to bring their address book with them. At the party, ask if you can send one to ten of their friends a letter or email, telling them about your book. Make sure you mention the name of the person who gave you the address.

Cookout—If you know someone giving a cookout, ask the host if you can have a book signing.

Helpful Non-Traditional Book Signing Tips:

- ➢ Think out-of-the box. All places are opportunities for having a book signing. Your risk is that you'll get a yes or no answer when asking if you can have one.

- ➢ Ask about leaving your book on display if you can't have a book signing.

- ➢ Ask to leave your business card along with other cards that are either posted or displayed.

CHAPTER 9
ANNOUCING EVENTS

An easy, free way to tell people about your events such as book signings, and interviews is to post them on Internet sites. By doing so, people you don't know will learn about your events.

Before posting on these sites, you may have to do the following requirements.

- ✓ Create an account

- ✓ Upload the details of the event

Below are some free Internet sites where authors can post their events.

Authors and Experts—www.authorsandexperts.com.

Upcoming Events—www.upcoming.org

Eventful—www.eventful.com

Craigslist—www.craigslist.com

✓ Listing events on Craigslist can only remain on it for two weeks.

Your Website—post the events on your website.

Author Websites—ask authors to post your event on their website and you will do the same for their event.

Instagram—www.instragram.com

✓ Post a picture of you or your book and mention the upcoming event, stating when, where, and time.

Facebook—www.facebook.com

✓ Post a picture of you or your book and mention the upcoming event, stating when, where, and time.

Goodreads—www.goodreads.com

✓ Must be a member to post your events.

Authorsden—www.authorsden.com

✓ Must be a published author and member to post your events.

CHAPTER 10
TRADITIONAL BOOK SIGNINGS

The most common marketing strategy for authors is to have a book signing at a bookstore. The event will cost the author's time and a specific percentage of book sale goes to the bookstore.

Helpful Bookstore Signing Tips:

- ➤ Independent and used bookstores are more receptive to allowing self-published authors to having a book signing.

- ➤ Small, independent, and used bookstores will not pre-order books. Authors will have to bring their books to sell on the day of the book signing.

Before authors have a book signing at a bookstore, develop a relationship with the owner and staff by doing a variety of things.

- ✓ Ask the bookstore owner to feature your book and see how well it sells.

- ✓ Visit the store often so you can talk to customers. Authors might ask what types of books people read. If the opportunity presents itself, authors can discuss their book.

- ✓ Create your own author and book buzz by having a monthly bookstore drawing or contest.

- ✓ Leave bookmarks or flyers at the bookstore as a give-away to people buying books.

Book Signing Success—Book signings can discourage an author. They are time consuming and boring. The author may sell no books or only a few after sitting for three hours. According to research, if an author sells one book, it's considered a success.

Below are suggestions that may help authors to have a successful book signing.

- ✓ Send out letters, postcards, or email blasts. Make sure you tell people the location, day, and time of the book signing.

- ✓ Schedule a newspaper interview before the book signing.

- ✓ Have a contest before or during the book signing.

Authors should do a variety of things to prepare for the book signing.

- ✓ Bring business cards, bookmarks, and flyers to the bookstore and ask if you can leave them on the counter near the cashier.

- ✓ Ask if you can put a flyer of the event in the window or on the front door.

- ✓ Create a poster with authors putting their picture, book and other pertinent book signing information on it. Authors should ask if they can leave the poster before the upcoming event.

Helpful Bookstore Tips:

- ➤ Authors should bring an easel to hold the poster.

- ➤ Ask nearby businesses if you can leave bookmarks or flyers.

- ➤ Have a friend pass out flyers the day of the book signing as people enter the bookstore.

Helpful Book Signing Tips:

- ➤ **<u>Jazz up the table</u>**—select a tablecloth color that accents your books. Bring objects such as balloons and flowers to bring attention to your table.

- ➤ **<u>Offer food or candy</u>**—helps draw people to your table. If you're selling a cookbook, consider giving away a sample from one of the recipes.

- **Make an interesting table**—visit bookstore signing for ideas. If possible, authors should work the theme of their book on the display.

- **Talk to people**—don't just sit behind a pile of books. Talk to individuals and ask questions. If you've written a romance book, you can ask, "What romance stories interest you?" "Who are your favorite romance authors?"

- **Give Away**—give everybody a business card, chapter sample or flyer even if the individual doesn't buy your book.

Have a contest—It's better to make the contest related to the author's book. If not, below are ideas that authors can create for contests.

- ✓ Give away raffle tickets, put them in a jar, and draw one. Suggestions for contest prizes are concert tickets, store coupon, or movie passes.

- ✓ Have people guess the number jellybeans in the jar and the person who guesses the closest number is the winner.

Helpful Contest Tips:

- ➤ Have people put their names on the back of the raffle ticket and collect names for expanding the authors' Contact List.

- ➤ State what's the prize for the individual who wins the contest.

- ➤ Say whether the person has to be present to win the contest.

Accept a variety of payment—At events, authors should accept a variety of payments. If not, authors will miss a chance to sell books.

- ✓ Cash.

- ✓ Checks.

- ✓ Credit cards.

Helpful Payment Tips:

- ➤ Authors should sign up for a free credit card device such as SquareUp or PayPal, making it possible for the author to accept credit card payments. The companies will charge a small processing fee.

➢ Authors need computers, iPhones, iPad2s, iPods, or Android Phones to use the credit card machines. Before the devices will work, authors must have an Internet connection.

➢ Bring extra dollars and coins so you can give people change when they pay by cash.

CHAPTER 11
SPEAKING ENGAGEMENTS

Not everyone feels comfortable doing public speaking. If you believe in your book, it should give you confidence to talk in front of an audience. Below are hints to help an author when invited to speak to a group.

- ✓ Practice what you want to say in front of a mirror.

- ✓ Prepare your speech and give it in front of two or three friends. Pick individuals that will give you honest feedback with suggestions for improvement.

- ✓ Join Toastmasters that will help you hone your speaking skills.

- ✓ Write what you want to say.

- ✓ Use a tape recorder and record your speech. You should listen to it and make notes on how to improve your talk.

- ✓ Attend venues where authors are speaking and learn from them.

If you're ready to conquer your fears of public speaking, look for speaking opportunities no matter where you live.

- ✓ Churches
- ✓ Class Reunions
- ✓ Family Reunions
- ✓ Libraries
- ✓ Social Clubs
- ✓ Cruise Ships

Once you find places to speak, you need to do a variety of activities.

- ✓ Identify the contact person.
- ✓ Send an informational package to the contact person. Give items such as bio, your book information, and website.
- ✓ Send the contact person a book.

If you're not successful in getting a speaking engagement at one of the these places, consider the following suggestions.

- ✓ Create an event, select a topic and be the speaker.

- ✓ Visit a public library and volunteer to hold a discussion on a specific topic.

- ✓ Offer to read books at venues such as the libraries, schools, day-care facilities, and nursing homes.

- ✓ Host an event, choose a writing topic and ask other authors to be guest speakers.

Helpful Speaking Engagement Tips:

- ➢ Speaking engagements help authors gain publicity, name recognition, and improve speaking and presentation skills.

- ➢ Gives authors an opportunity to gain addresses to build their contact list.

- ➢ Let authors know they can sell their books when you sponsor an event.

- ➢ Ask if you can sell your books after a speaking engagement.

- Volunteer as a guest speaker at venues such as but not limited to conference panels, book expos, and class courses.

CHAPTER 12
BOOK EVENTS

Authors are always looking for events to sell their books, gain exposure, and find opportunities to showcase their works. Below are ways to find them.

Book Clubs—Below are places where authors can find book clubs.

- ✓ Churches
- ✓ Retirement Communities
- ✓ Libraries
- ✓ Women's Groups

Helpful Book Club Tips:

- ➢ Prepare for the book discussion so you can answer questions.
- ➢ Write at least 5-10 book questions that will generate discussion.

> Make all your books available to sell even though you are discussing one specific book. People may want to buy your other books.

Websites—Two popular websites with information that gives a list of book fairs, events, etc. where authors can find places to sell books.

- ✓ www.loc.gov/loc/cfbook/bookfair

- ✓ www.bookfairs.com

CHAPTER 13
ENTICING POTENTIAL BUYERS

Authors should be innovative when getting people to buy their books. Find ways that you can use on a repeated basis.

Hold a contest—Authors should use their imagination to create a contest. They can give away prizes such as free books, gift certificates, and discounts. Below are suggestions for a contest.

- ✓ Have individuals suggest a book cover for your upcoming book.

- ✓ Give a prize to the person who has the best question of the month. Authors make sure you answer everyone's question.

- ✓ Have people explain why the book makes a good series.

- ✓ Give away an autographed book to the first five people who leave a message on your website saying why they want to read your book.

Give away free books—Everyone wants something free. Authors should watch for opportunities to give their book away,

- ✓ Give a book to the person who asked you to speak at a book club.

- ✓ Donate a book for door prizes.

- ✓ Exchange a book with other authors and ask for a review and you'll do the same.

- ✓ Take part in an author's give-away program that lasts for a specific time.

Allow readers to sample your book—Everyone likes to see what they're buying. The book synopsis may not be enough to interest a person to buy it. A chapter excerpt may entice them.

Helpful Sample Book Tips:

Create a book chapter excerpt and give it away free. Authors should make an easy to carry trifold brochure for your chapter.

Leave book chapters in a variety of places where people gather.

- ✓ Doctor/Dentist offices

- ✓ Laundromats

- ✓ Beauty and barber shops

- ✓ Airplanes (put in seat pockets)

- ✓ Airports, bus and train terminals

- ✓ Hotel rooms

- ✓ Car dealership waiting room

Give discounts—Everyone loves a discount and below are suggestions for giving them.

- ✓ Give people a discount coupon on the day of the book signing.

- ✓ Offer a discount when someone buys one or more books.

- ✓ Give a discount coupon to people who signed up for your upcoming book release.

Develop a book series—When writing your novel, consider whether your plot could be a series. During or at the end of the book, leave people wondering what transpired to a particular character or situation. An author hopes they will want to learn what happened and will ask if you are writing another book.

- ✓ Sell your books as a series and bundle them for a discount

CHAPTER 14
PROMOTING WHILE TRAVELING

Authors who travel can promote their book. Be imaginative and leave a book in a variety of places.

Cruises—On every cruise ship, there's a library.

- ✓ Put your book in the ship's library.

- ✓ Leave a book, flyer, or business card in the cabin.

Helpful Tips:

- ➢ Don't ask for permission, go to the cruise ship library and put your book in it

- ➢ Ask relatives, friends, or neighbors that cruise to put your book in the cruise ship's library.

Airplanes—Every airplane has a seat pocket.

- ✓ Leave your book, bookmark, or flyer in the seat pocket.

Helpful Airplane Tip:

- ➢ Be sure to put it between the airplane magazines. If not, the airplane cleaning crew will throw the book, bookmark, or flyer away.

Hotels—Every hotel has nightstands where you might find a Bible left by the Gideons.

- ✓ Leave a book, flyer, or bookmark in the same nightstand as the Gideon Bible.

Resorts—Leave a book in the room's bedroom nightstand or anywhere in the room.

Helpful Travel Tips:

If authors don't want to pack and bring a book with them, they can follow the below suggestions.

- ➢ Give away or leave business cards.

- ➢ Bring bookmarks or flyers that can authors can leave or give away.

If you plan on staying in a place for a few days, weeks, or months, consider the following suggestions.

- ✓ Ask if you can have a book signing.

- ✓ Volunteer to speak at a public or private library.

✓ Arrange an interview with local newspapers, radio, or television stations.

CHAPTER 15
LIBRARIES

United States and foreign countries have libraries. Authors can put their books in libraries to gain exposure and receive name recognition.

Authors might ask why give their book to a library. It's easy and below are several reasons.

- ✓ When individuals like a book, they might buy others written by the author.

- ✓ Individuals reading books they like, may recommend it to others.

- ✓ If libraries receive enough requests for an author's book, they might order it.

Authors might consider putting their books in the following libraries.

➢ **Public libraries**

➢ **Private libraries**

- ✓ Retirement communities
- ✓ Nursing homes
- ✓ Church libraries
- ✓ Cruise ship libraries
- ✓ Day care facilities if you have a children's book
- ✓ School libraries—public and private
- ✓ College libraries
- ✓ Prisons

Helpful Library Tips:

➢ To put your books in public libraries can be easy but ask if they have guidelines and follow them.

➢ Ask out-of-town relatives and friends to put your book in their local libraries, public and private. If they don't think they can do it, ask for the library contact person and you can do it on your own.

➢ Contact public or private libraries yourself and ask for the procedures for an author to put a book in the library.

CHAPTER 16
ASK FOR HELP

Authors may not want to admit it but selling books is a business. Successful entrepreneurs aren't afraid to ask for help and neither should authors. Don't be afraid to ask relatives and friends for help. They will either say "yes" or "no."

Your relatives and friends may not buy your book, but they can help sell your book. Relatives and friends can help in many ways.

Book review—Give relatives and friends your book to read and ask them to post a review.

Bookmarks/flyers—Give relatives and friends bookmarks they can give to people or leave in bookstores, libraries, businesses, etc.

Business cards—Give relatives and friends business cards they can give to people or leave in bookstores, libraries, and businesses.

Discussions—Ask relatives and friends to tell avid readers you're an author.

Book club recommendation—If relatives and friends belong to a book club, ask if they'll recommend your book for their book choice of the month.

Facebook/Instagram/Tweeter—For relatives and friends who have Facebook, Instagram, and Tweeter accounts, ask them to post pictures of your book or other book events.

Loan books—Give your relatives and friends your book and ask them to loan it to their friends, co-workers, and neighbors. Inside the book, put a flyer or bookmark with a list of your books and website.

Relatives/friends traveling—Give your relatives and friends a book, bookmarks, or business cards if they're going on a trip and ask them to leave it on an airplane, hotel, and resort.

Sell your book—Ask relatives and friends to sell your book and you will give them a small commission. For every book sold, you'll give them two dollars.

Neighborhood Book Signing—Ask relatives and friends if they'll host a neighborhood book signing party where you can discuss and sell your book.

Guest Speaker—If your relatives and friends belong to clubs or organizations, volunteer as a guest speaker at their meetings.

Contests—Ask relatives and friends to tell people when you're having a contest. Have them spread the word on Facebook, Instagram, and Tweeter

Spread the word—Ask relatives and friends to tell people when you'll be at a book signing or other event.

Earn money—Suggest relatives and friends who have websites or blogs to enroll in Amazon's affiliate program and they can earn money by adding links to your books.

CHAPTER 17
AUTHOR WEBSITE

I'm still surprised at the number of published authors that don't have a website. It's essential to have one and if an author doesn't have one, they are missing opportunities to market, promote, and sell books.

Some authors wonder if they really need a website because it's time-consuming to maintain one. Below are some reasons of how a website can help an author.

- ✓ Provides opportunities to market, promote, and sell books.

- ✓ Develops a channel for authors to connect with and communicate with readers and fans.

- ✓ Gives people a chance to learn about the author and their books.

- ✓ Promotes an author's book signing events.

- ✓ Offer a newsletter to keep in touch with the authors' readers and fans.

- ✓ Sells authors' books and related merchandise.

- ✓ Makes an author's information available to the media.

An Author's Website—Authors can create their websites or hire a professional. Authors can practice creating a website using the following free ones. Most of the websites are user friendly and offer other services for a fee such as ad free and marketing.

- ✓ Freewebs—www.freewebs.com

- ✓ Weebly—www.weebly.com

- ✓ Wix—www.wix.com

- ✓ WordPress—www.wordpress

Helpful Free Website Tips:

- ➢ Preview your website before publishing it.

- ➢ Use the tutorial to help create a website.

- ➢ Understand that the website is free but they offer additional services for a fee.

➢ Review other author websites and get ideas to help you decide on what to include or how you might design your pages.

Website Pages—authors don't have to make their website elaborate. Keep it simple but informative. You can add as many pages as you want. Make sure you include these pages.

✓ **About Me**—page provides people with author information.

✓ **Books**—dedicate this page for your books and synopsis.

✓ **Contact Information**—contact page allows people to leave messages.

✓ **Book Review Page**—people can read the reviews left by individuals who read your books.

Helpful Author Website Tips:

➢ Buy a domain name to make your website unique to you. You can buy a domain name from the website you're using or from websites that sell domain names. The cost varies and can start from $20.00 a year to $150.00 or more.

➢ Update the author website at least once a month.

➢ Include a free newsletter to give people information on your next book release, insight into your writing skills and events.

➢ Sponsor contests and give away prizes such as an autographed book, tickets, and discounts.

➢ Create links to other author websites, blogs, and social media sites.

➢ Include keywords to your website.

CHAPTER 18
AUTHOR FRIENDLY WEBSITES

There are many free sites for authors to market, promote, or sell books. Before authors can upload books, add information, and post pictures they must set up an account.

Many friendly author websites allow published authors to advertise their book, write blogs, sell books, etc. for "free." A list below gives the names of friendly author websites.

AuthorsDen, www.authorsden.com—This site has free and fee services for authors to post biographies, books, sample chapters, sell books, write blogs, etc.

GoodReads, www.goodreads.com—Authors can set up an Author's Page, ask readers to list books on Listopia, advertise, give books away, lead a question-and-answer group book discussion, etc.

Awesome Gang, www.awesomegang.com—Awesome Gang Newsletter is a free tool to help authors with marketing but it takes three weeks to receive it. Authors can upload their books and have access to one of the best available book email lists. For a cost, the site guarantees the author a spot on the home page and various social media promotions.

Discount Book Man, www.discountbookman.com—A site where authors can promote their book for a fee and have it put on the front page for five days.

Book Bongos, www.bookbongo.com—A free and fee book promotion site for authors.

Book Daily, www.bookdaily.com—Authors can share one of their book chapters for free and reach a large audience.

Lovely Book Promotion, this site is located at www.lovelybookpromotions.com—According to this site, authors can gain exposure to over 9,000 Facebook Fans, over 20,000 Twitter followers, and hundreds of website visitors. Without a charge, authors can receive publicity, reviews, and interviews.

Book Prasier, found at www.bookprasier.com—Provides multiple ways for authors to sell their books.

Bublish.com, www.bublish.com--Authors can use the free and paid versions of Bublish to write, promote, and sell books.

Helpful Author Website Tips:

- Visit the sites often to make sure the requirements haven't changed.

- Continue to search for author friendly websites that can help authors market, promote, and sell their books.

CHAPTER 19
AUTHOR WEBSITE MARKETING

Authors that aren't comfortable marketing, promoting, and selling their book, can use their author's website address. It's subtle but effective.

A website address gives authors a chance to do effortless yet efficient marketing. Authors' website addresses are better recognized as the Uniform Resource Locator, URL. My address is www.lorrainemharris.com.

Below are ideas authors can do that are easy and not time consuming.

- ✓ Add the URL in the author's book.

- ✓ Put the author's URL on business cards.

- ✓ Insert the author's URL in your email signature line.

- ✓ Affix the author's URL on handout materials such as flyers, bookmarks, and chapter excerpts.

- ✓ Include author's URL to your voicemail.

- ✓ Add your URL to outgoing correspondence.

- ✓ Write a check to pay bills, make donations, give as a check and add your URL.

- ✓ Submit your URL to free search engines that submit it to directories and other search engines. A site where authors can submit their URL—www.addme.com to help drive traffic to an author's website.

CHAPTER 20
SUCCESSFUL BLOGGING

Authors who blog have a voice. They can discuss issues such as their writing and marketing experiences. Authors that blog can drive traffic to their websites because it gives people a reason to make return visits.

To create a blog is easy and if you have a website, most of them give you a Blog Page. If not, authors can find many free sites to develop a Blog. Below are a few free ones.

- ✓ www.wordpress.com

- ✓ www.blogger.com

- ✓ www.wix.com

- ✓ www.weebly.com

Once authors find a site, they're ready to start blogging but you must do the following steps.

- ✓ Sign up for a free Blog and set up an account.

- ✓ Pick a template.

- ✓ Select a name for your Blog.

- ✓ Write a blog.

- ✓ Preview your blog before posting it.

- ✓ Share your blog on such media sites such as Twitter, Linkedin, and Instagram.

The following are effective suggestions that can help authors become a successful blogger.

Be interesting—Make sure you keep your readers' attention by giving them new and fresh information.

Get your point across—Have a purpose and stick to it. Be passionate when writing your blog and give readers a reason to look forward to reading the blog.

Keep up steam—Once you blog and they find people interested in what you have to say, you must blog often.

Use Images—Pictures are powerful tools. The right image can grab a reader's attention causing them to read your blog.

Make Friends with Other Bloggers—Find other bloggers' websites and do things such as make comments, ask for an interview, and join the conversation. These activities will get your name in more places and it might generate more traffic to the author's website.

Keywords—Make keywords the core of your blog. Find out what people are reading, but don't let keywords be your driving force.

Be committed—You have to invest time and be consistent writing your blog or your readers will lose interest,

Link to social media—After you blog, make sure you link it to social media such as Twitter, Facebook, and Instagram.

Helpful Blogging Tips:

- ➢ Write a blog on a regular basis.

- ➢ Interview authors and post on your blog.

- ➢ Write blogs based on topics such as writing, publishing, and editing.

- ➢ Link your blog to other blogs and websites.

- ➢ Add keywords to your blog.

CHAPTER 21
SOCIAL MEDIA IDEAS

Social media is still new to most authors. It's a continuous work in progress. Besides linking social media to other websites, authors don't know much else to do.

Through research, I've learned many ideas that other authors are doing on social media. Listed are things I've found helpful.

- ✓ Make your fan page your main page on Facebook.

- ✓ Bring your book alive by showing props from a book chapter. If your book mentions a particular restaurant, you might show a copy of their menu.

- ✓ Provide details of your upcoming book event.

- ✓ Give insights of your writing process.

- ✓ Take a picture of your writing space.

- ✓ Keep your fans up-to-date on the progress of your new book.
- ✓ Discuss the roadblocks to writing.

- ✓ Post a quote from your book.

- ✓ Discuss books you're reading and write a review.

- ✓ Share your music playlist.

- ✓ Create a summer reading list.

- ✓ Show pictures of your pets with one of your books and post it.

- ✓ Take a picture of someone reading your book and post it.

- ✓ Find inspirational writing quotes and post them.

- ✓ Post writing quotes.

CHAPTER 22
KEYWORDS

After creating a website or Blog, most authors forget to add keywords and phrases to their Search Engine Optimization (SEO). SEO is the process for increasing the quality and quantity of driving traffic to an author's Website or Blog.

It's important to add keywords and phrases because that's what makes it possible for people when they search the Internet to find your website and Blog. Think about the keywords that a person might enter in the search box to find your book.

Remember when selecting keywords, they are for getting your book to show up in searches. It isn't easy to pick the right words for people to find your book because they're searching by genre, your name, or at random.

Finding the most effective keywords is hard because they're limited to five to seven words. You want the widest access to more categories and here are ideas that might help.

Helpful Keyword Tips:

- Find successful selling books in the same genre such as romance, mystery, and children. Look at the keywords used by those authors.

- Pick keywords associated with a celebrity or a famous person. The word must be an accurate presentation of the person and you had to do more than mention the celebrity or famous person's name in your novel.

- Choose keywords based on your novel's setting such as in Maine, the Ritz Hotel, or football stadium.

CHAPTER 23
SCHEDULING SOCIAL MEDIA

Although social media is a necessity for authors, it can be time-consuming and overwhelming. Social media can be easier if you use tools that automate the scheduling. What does that mean?

Authors should use vehicles that allow them to schedule their blog posts and tweets. Many free sites help authors to make social media easier to manage by pre-scheduling the days and times for these activities.

Twuffer, www.twuffer.com—a site where authors use with their Twitter account to schedule tweets. Set up the account and it allows an author to compose and schedule 50 tweets a month.

Buffer, www.buffer.com—authors can schedule posts, track the performance, and manage accounts in one place.

IFTTT, www.ifttt.com—a tool for authors to schedule blog posts for their Facebook page.

Pagemodo, www.pagemodo.com--authors can pick free Facebook templates, schedule posts, and design social media photos.

Websites—depending on your website, it might have a feature that allows authors to schedule posts to social media sites.

CHAPTER 24
BOOK REVIEWS

One of the most difficult challenges authors continue to face is getting people to post reviews of their book. There's no foolproof way to get your book reviewed.

A review can boost an author's confidence and help sell your books. Below are some suggestions that may work.

Author reviews—Give your book to a published author and ask for a review.

Exchange reviews--Offer to give a review to an author and in exchange they do the same for you.

Relatives, friends, and neighbors—Any relative, friend, and neighbor that bought your book, ask them to write a review.

Blog readers—Ask blog readers for a review and offer an incentive such as a free copy of your next book, discount, and prizes.

Book review request—On the last page of your book, thank the reader and ask for a review.

Helpful Book Review Tips:

- Have a page on your website where people can leave a review.

- Post all reviews on your website but ask for permission before posting them.

- Ask other authors how they have had success in getting book reviews.

CHAPTER 25
SPECIAL OCCASION SELLING

Some authors may not realize it, but every occasion is an opportunity to market, promote, and sell your book. Below are ways to sell and give away your books.

Birthdays—Give your book to your relatives, friends, and neighbors as a gift. Suggest they buy your book and give to someone as a birthday gift.

Hospitals—Authors can give their book to someone having to spend more than a few days in the hospital.

Rehab Facilities—People in rehab facilities can become bored when spending weeks of recovery, give them a book.

Christmas—A book can be a special gift for relatives, friends, or neighbors who have everything.

Valentine's Day—Do something nice for someone, give them a single rose and one of your books.

Anniversary—First year is paper. Suggest to men that he give his wife a romance novel along with a special gift that will show his wife that he is thoughtful, romantic, and enduring. A wife could give her husband a book along with another gift.

Baby Shower—Buy a gift for the baby and give the mother-to-be one of your books.

Hostess Gift—If you're visiting someone, leave one of your books along with a thank you note for their hospitality.

Travelers—Someone you know may be taking a trip. Give your book them to read if they're going to the beach, on a long airplane flight, a cruise, or car trip.

Retirement—Give your book to someone retiring.

Bachelorette Party—Give a romance novel to the bride-to-be, maid-of-honor, or the bridesmaids.

Door Prizes—Authors have so many opportunities to give their books away as door prizes, at book signings, and book clubs.

Helpful Door Prize Tip:

➤ Put together a basket and make the contents of it relevant to your book. For example, I made a basket and filled it with my book, *Sunday Golf*, a sleeve of golf balls, golf tees, and a golf towel.

CHAPTER 26
ADVERTISING OPPORTUNITIES

Advertisement can be expensive. I had to find ways to advertise my books without breaking the bank. Authors should take advantage of unusual places to advertise. Below are some different places that authors may not have considered.

Church bulletin—Call the church and see if they sell ads. Many Catholic churches sell bulletin ads.

Club/organization advertisements—Buy a full page, half page, quarter page, or business card advertisement when clubs or organizations sponsor fund raising events and are looking for patrons.

Patron—Become a patron for a golf tournament. The club or organization sponsoring the tournament look for people or companies to buy a hole on the golf course. You can put whatever you want on the sign.

Helpful Patron Tips:

- ➢ Become a patron for a golf tournament. On the golf course tee box, golfers will see the signs. Below is what my placard read when I was a patron for a golf tournament hole.

Lorraine M. Harris, Author
www.lorrainemharris.com

- ➢ Watch in the paper or talk to golfers about any upcoming golf tournaments. Contact the club or organization and find out how you can become a patron.

Funeral Homes—Buy an advertisement on the back of funeral home fans.

Merchandise—Create merchandise such as T-Shirts, mugs, and pens.

Helpful Merchandise Tip:

- ➢ Put your URL on all merchandise.

Tissue box advertisement—Design a tissue box, featuring your books. It costs five dollars at www.mykleenextissue.com.

Helpful Tissue Box Tip:

- Ask medical, business offices, etc. if you can leave a tissue box in the waiting area.

Enter Contests—Identify legitimate contests where you can enter your work. Many are listed in the Writer's Market Manual, Writer's Digest Magazine, and other publications.

If you win a contest, there are some positive benefits.

- ✓ A contest validates an author's work when becoming a winner.

- ✓ An author can use the title, "Award winning author."

- ✓ Mention your achievement on your author profiles, websites, and bio.

Helpful Contests Tips:

- Verify that the contest is legitimate.

- Determine contests costs.

- Read the rules and follow them.

> Can receive useful feedback when entering contests. Many of the judges are agents, publishers, published authors, editors, etc.

Address Return Labels—Create return address labels with a picture of your book beside your name and address, along with your website address.

Helpful Address Label Tip:

> Put your return address label on all outgoing mail.

Donate Magazines—Before donating used magazines, replace the subscription mailing address label with your author return address one.

Helpful Donation Tip:

> Donate used magazines to doctor and dentist offices, beauty and barber shops, etc.

CHAPTER 27
CONNECT WITH PEOPLE

Authors should continue to meet new people to build their contact list and to talk about their book. One of the easiest ways to make this happen is to become "a joiner."

How? Do what you like or do something new. Below are chances for authors to meet people.

<u>Hobbies</u>—What is your hobby? If you don't have one, try something new and meet people.

<u>Sports</u>—If you enjoy participating in sports such as bowling, golfing, and tennis, you can meet people. This also applies to attending football, basketball, and baseball games. You never know when you may meet someone who likes to read books.

<u>Clubs/Organizations</u>—Join a club or organization that may interest you and meet people.

<u>Book Clubs</u>—Most authors enjoy reading when they aren't writing. Join a book club and learn insight into what people are reading and why.

Exercise—Join an athletic club but it will cost. If you don't want the expense, do an exercise that's free such as walking, swimming, cycling, and dancing. These groups may socialize after exercising, giving you an opportunity to learn what other activities people are doing.

Travel—Join a travel club that goes on multi-day trips. Take along one of your books and depending on the length of the trip, loan it to one traveler to read. That person might create a buzz, causing others to read the book while on the trip and buy your other books.

Games—If you enjoy playing games such as Mah Jongg, Trivia, and darts, play and meet people.

Volunteer—There are lots of opportunities to volunteer your services and meet a variety of people.

Writing Groups—To hone skills, offer your help, and share information. Authors joining a writing group will meet other authors, learn from their experiences, and hone their skills.

Helpful People Connect Tips:

- ➢ Remember your main goal is to meet new people. Your second goal is to let people know you're an author.

- Take a friend to these events and have them tell people you're an author.

CHAPTER 28
NETWORK WITH AUTHORS

Networking with other authors is one of the best ways to keep motivated, learn more about writing, publishing, and marketing. Remember, authors are colleagues, not competitors. Make them your allies.

Join a writing group—As an author you want to continue improving your skills and meeting other authors that can help you and vice versa. Some benefits of joining a writing group.

- ✓ Improve listening skills.
- ✓ Develop critiquing skills.
- ✓ Hone writing skills.
- ✓ Network with authors.
- ✓ Gain name recognition.
- ✓ Become a recognized expert in certain areas.

- ✓ Offer your help to authors.

Form a coalition with other authors—Other authors know people you don't and vice versa. Form a coalition by identifying authors who will promote your work with the understanding you'll do the same.

Authors can do this in several ways. Below are examples of what you can do when forming an alliance with another author.

- ✓ Participate in book signing events and put other author business cards, flyers, and chapter excerpts on your table when that author can't attend the event.

- ✓ Give author's business cards, flyers, and chapter excerpts away when you're traveling.

- ✓ Take an author's book when you cruise and put it in the ship's library.

- ✓ Recognize other published authors when giving speeches, having a party, or teaching a course.

- ✓ Talk about other author events on your website.

- ✓ Post book signing events on social media such as Facebook, Tweeter, and Instagram.

Attend writing conferences—An opportunity to meet individuals such as authors, editors, and publishers.

Social media—If you can't find authors to network with in your area, look on social media sites such as Facebook and Tweeter for author forums. Find authors with the same interest and send them an email. Start slow and build a relationship.

CHAPTER 29
SUPPORT AUTHORS

Marketing, promoting, and selling your book is important, but it's also imperative to connect with and support other authors. If you support other authors they will do the same. Below are ways to assist other authors.

Attend book signing events—Attend book signing events to show your support.

Helpful Book Event Tip:

> ➤ Help create a buzz by talking to people attending the event and mention the authors' books and where the authors have their tables.

Write reviews—Read an author's book and give a review.

Helpful Review Tips:

> ➤ Write a review and post it either on their website or on sites where authors sell their books.

> Tell the author you've written a review and where you posted it.

Provide your expertise—If you have skills in editing, proofreading, or formatting books, offer your assistance to authors.

Volunteer—Locate book signing events and see if they need volunteers. Look into possibilities such as conferences, charity events, and book expos.

Create links—If you have a website, you can provide a link to other author websites.

Share writing skills—Consider sponsoring a writing/critique group. Forming a group, benefits you and other authors by honing writing, listening, and critiquing skills.

Mentor a writer—Provide assistance to someone new to writing.

Book clubs—Recommend an author's book to book clubs.

Business cards—Give authors' business cards to people.

CHAPTER 30
BUSINESS CARDS

Business cards are probably the easiest and cheapest way to market and promote your book. Every author should have business cards and carry them to give away everywhere.

Below are some ideas for getting business cards.

- ✓ Make business cards using computer software. Depending on the card size and quality, they can cost as low as $3.99 for 100 cards.

- ✓ Buy business cards from places that make them such as Staples, Office Depot, and a variety of websites. VistaPrint (www.vistaprint.com) is one of the cheapest places to buy them.

- ✓ Obtain free business cards if you're an active or retired military person. Visit the website, www.militarybenefits.com for details.

Daily, discover ways to give your business card away or leave it somewhere. Below are some ideas to how authors can use business cards to market, promote, and sell their books.

Meeting people—Give a business card to everyone you meet.

Relatives and Friends—Give business cards to relatives and friends—an easy way for them to tell people you're an author.

Bulletin Boards—Post a business card on bulletin boards. Look for bulletins in grocery stores, laundromats, restaurants, and other places where people leave their cards.

Paying Bills—If you still pay bills the old fashion way, put your business card in the envelope when sending off your payment.

Donating Money—Make a donation to charity by sending a check in the mail and put your business card in the envelope.

Restaurant—When you go to breakfast, lunch, or dinner and before giving the menu back to the waiter, paperclip your business card to a page.

Restaurant Give Away—Some restaurants have bowls where they have drawings, don't forget to drop your card inside.

Paying Restaurant Bill—Pay your restaurant bill and put your business card inside the folder.

Unsolicited Advertisements—When you receive information from banks, credit card companies, and magazine renewals, put your business card inside the postage paid envelope and return it to the sender.

Offices—Paperclip your business card inside of magazines at any office such as doctor, dentist, and car dealerships.

Give a Discount—Tell someone about a book signing event, give them a business card and on the back give them a discount.

Accolades—On the back of your business card and before you leave it some place, write a glowing review of your book by saying something such as "Here's the book I've been telling you about." "A must-read book." "An awesome book." "This book is worth reading."

Helpful Business Card Tips:

- Put your picture on your business card for recognition.

- Carry your business card with you.

- Take paperclips and thumb tacks with you. You'll use them to attach to magazines and post on bulletin boards.

- Leave the back of business cards blank so you can write things such as discounts, book signing events, and glowing review messages.

CHAPTER 31
BOOK FLYERS

Authors can use book flyers like business cards. They are an easy and cheap way to market and promote your book. Every author should carry them and use these ideas for giving away book flyers.

Make or buy book flyers.

- ✓ Make the book flyer into a trifold. It's easier to carry.

- ✓ Put the picture of your book on the book flyer, how to buy it, and website URL.

- ✓ Add a synopsis and a chapter excerpt on the flyer.

Discover ways to give your book flyer away. Below are ideas on how to use them to market, promote, and sell your books. Don't get offended if the person you try to give a flyer to says, "No thank you."

Waiting Rooms—Offer people a flyer when you see them reading a book in offices of doctors, dentists, or emergency rooms.

Airports—Offer people a flyer when you see them reading a book.

Airplanes—Place a flyer in the magazines in the seat pocket. If the person sitting beside you is reading a book, give him or her a flyer.

Hotels—Leave a flyer in the nightstand or inside the Gideon Bible.

Restaurant—Put a flyer in a menu.

Unsolicited Advertisements—When you receive information from banks, credit card companies and magazine renewals, put your flyer inside the postage paid envelope and return it to the sender.

CHAPTER 32
AUTHOR VISIBILITY

Authors don't always think of ways they can gain visibility. Photos help people to recognize authors.

To get visibility is easier than most authors think. Below are easy ways to do it and it will cost nothing.

- ✓ Ask readers to post pictures of them reading your book.

- ✓ Contact the local newspaper and ask for an interview.

- ✓ Create a video and upload to social media sites such as YouTube, Facebook, and Instagram.

- ✓ Take pictures at a variety of events that you attend such as charity events, tournaments and post to social media sites.

- ✓ Accept offers to have your picture taken by a newspaper reporter or individuals.

- Volunteer for activities that aren't author related, have your picture taken, and post it.

Helpful Author Visibility Tips:

- Carry a camera or use your cell phone to take pictures.

- Ask others for copies of pictures they took at an event you attended.

- Post pictures on your website and social media sites such as Facebook, Instagram, and YouTube.

- Provide pictures to your local newspapers of events that may interest their readers.

CHAPTER 33
BOOK ENDORSEMENTS

Authors should consider getting a celebrity, a famous person, or a professional in a specific field to endorse their book. Getting a high-profile individual to give or review your book can make a difference in selling it.

If feasible, include the celebrity or famous person in your book. You ask, who are these individuals?

- ✓ Look beyond people you know. Make a list of individuals that might fit in your storyline. You wrote a book on child safety, contact an active or retired police officer, firefighter, and teacher.

- ✓ Contact people such as congress members, heads of associations, local and national celebrities, company presidents, prominent authors, and reporters.

Do the following before you finish your book.

- ✓ Take the time to find addresses and send a letter to the person you want to endorse your book. Authors can find celebrity addresses on websites and at www.celebrity.addresses.com.

- ✓ Give the person a copy of the book you want them to endorse so they might read it. If the book cover is ready, send that too.

- ✓ Send the person a copy of your book when it's ready for release.

Most high-profile people are busy. You can make it easy for the individual by writing two, three sample endorsements and suggest they edit, rewrite, or write one of their own. When you write and give the person a draft endorsement letter, make sure it's well-written without errors.

Helpful Book Endorsement Tips:

- ➢ Put the quote, review, or endorsement on the back or inside your book.

- ➢ Include the quote, review, or endorsement on your promotional materials.

- ➢ Post the quote, review, or endorsement on your website or social media.

- ➢ Make sure you tell the individual the date when you need the endorsement.

- Follow-up on your inquiry if you haven't heard from the individual.
- Include a self-addressed, stamped envelope when you make your request.

- Send a thank you note.

CHAPTER 34
BOOK TESTIMONIALS

Why not get a testimonial from a famous author or local author? You say you don't know one.

It's great to shoot for the famous author but don't overlook local authors that have lots of people following them. When asking for a testimonial, avoid telling the author your life story. Don't beg or rant how your book is a best seller or it's your first one.

Authors who get testimonials from authors can add credibility to your book. Before you ask the author for a testimony, below are suggestions for getting one.

- ✓ Make a list of ten to twenty authors who write in your genre. Why do you need so many? The more you ask, the better your chances are in getting a testimonial.

- ✓ Don't be afraid to ask an author for a testimonial.

- ✓ If you want to shoot for the well-known authors, their contact information is available on their website, in their books, and newsletters.

Below is a sample of what you might write when contacting an author.

Hi (author name),

I read your (title of book) and liked it because…keep it brief.

This winter, I have a book that's coming out, published by (publishing company). Give the book's synopsis. I'm getting other testimonials for my book and would appreciate you considering giving me one. If you prefer, I can send you several chapters or the entire novel for your review.

I appreciate and thank you for your consideration,

Your Name

Author
Website Address

Helpful Book Testimonial Tips:

- ➢ Buy the author's book and start your note with a compliment, stating what you liked.

- Send other testimonials you might have received. It might give the author an incentive to write one.

- Write and send several well written sample testimonials that the author can edit and rewrite.

- Put the testimonial on the back of your book cover or inside your book.

- Include the testimonial on your promotional materials.

- Post the testimonial on your website.

- Make sure you give the author the date when you need the testimonial.

- Follow-up on your request if you haven't heard from the author.

- Include a self-addressed, stamped envelope so the author can return the testimony.

- Show your appreciation and send a thank you note.

CHAPTER 35
INTERVIEWS

Interviews can help authors gain publicity. Media interviews cost the author nothing with the benefits enormous. If you don't get the interview the first time you ask, keep trying.

Below are ideas where authors can ask for an interview.

Newspapers:

- ✓ Local newspapers and surrounding areas where you live that have an author or book column. Obtain the columnist's contact information and send him or her a copy of your book and mention you're available for an interview.

- ✓ Newspapers in other states that have an author or book column. Obtain the columnist's contact information and send him or her a copy of your book and mention you're available for an interview.

Magazines:

- ✓ Local magazines and surrounding areas where you live.

- ✓ Magazines in other states.

Helpful Magazine Interview Tip:

- ➢ Find a local magazine or newspaper and volunteer to write a onetime article that may land an interview.

Radio Stations:

- ✓ Find local radio stations that have a platform for interviewing authors.

- ✓ Research radio stations outside your locale that have a platform for interviewing authors. It helps if your book's setting takes place in a city within that locale.

Television Stations:

- ✓ Local cable television stations that interview authors.

- ✓ Television stations in other states that interview authors. It helps if your book's setting takes place in one of the cities in that state.

Helpful Interview Tips:

- Review your book and know the content in order to answer questions.

- Take notes before your interview.

- Make up interview questions and give them to the interviewer.

- Rehearse the answers to questions you think the interviewer might ask.

- Mention your website address during the interview.

- Mention details of any upcoming book events.

- State where people can buy your book.

- Try to schedule a book event before the interview and mention the information.

- Show your appreciation and send a note thanking the newspaper, radio or television stations' interviewer.

CHAPTER 36
WRITING EXPOSURE

Take every opportunity to obtain exposure. No matter what you write, it gives you a chance to connect with readers. Below are ideas to find ways to get exposure by using your writing skills.

Newsletters—Give away a newsletter on your author's website. It's a way to share personal insights, provide information to readers, and build your contact list. What can an author put in a newsletter?

- ✓ Book Update—Discuss your new book release.

- ✓ Life Highlights—Talk about your life such as how a trip gave you an idea for a book. You drink a particular coffee or tea while writing. You went out walking and saw two people holding hands and laughing and it inspired you to write a romance novel.

- ✓ Interviews—Interview an author in your genre.

- ✓ Reading Book List—Tell readers what book you're reading and provide them with a review.

- ✓ Events—Talk about upcoming events and recount your experiences.

Helpful Newsletter Tips:

- ➢ Use an email marketing service that helps authors design email newsletters, send them to your email list, and share it on social media. One such service is MailChimp, www.mailchimp.com.

- ➢ Send your newsletter out on a regular basis.

Newspapers—Research newspapers where you can write a onetime article or an on-going column. Below are where you can find newspapers.

- ✓ Local, community, and free newspapers.

- ✓ National newspapers.

Helpful Writing Exposure Tips:

- ➢ Volunteer to write a club newsletter to get experience.

- ➢ Write a newsletter with an author in your genre.

➢ National magazines—Research national magazines where you can write a onetime article or ongoing articles.

➢ Local magazines—Find local magazines where you can write a onetime article or ongoing articles.

➢ Magazines in your genre—Find magazines in your genre and write a onetime article or ongoing articles.

CHAPTER 37
BACK OF THE BOOK

At the end of the book, authors have an opportunity to market, promote, and sell their books. Listed below are numerous things authors can do in their book.

<u>Authors Books</u>—Make a list of your published books.

Helpful Author Book List Tips:

➢ Provide a link to where people can buy your books.

➢ Include your website address.

<u>Reviews</u>—Ask readers to leave a review on your website.

<u>Chapter excerpt from your next book</u>—Leave the book with a cliff-hanger or, if the book is part of a series. Put a chapter excerpt of your new book.

Helpful Back of the Book Tips:

- Thank the readers for reading your book.

- Ask readers to leave a review on your website or where they bought your book.

- Explain how the reader can pre-order your upcoming book.

- Tell readers where they can buy your book.

- Ask readers to lend your book to a friend. Word-of-mouth is an author's best publicity.

- Look at other authors' books and see how they use the back of their book to market, promote, and sell their books.

CHAPTER 38
SUCESSFUL MARKETING TIPS

Authors have no choice but to market, promote, and sell their books. While doing so, remember you are in control.

Ten ways to have success with your book.

- **Plan**—decide what strategies you want to use when marketing, promoting, and selling your book.

- **Positive**—be passionate when selling your book.

- **Proactive**—take the time to market, promote, and sell your book.

- **Prioritize**—decide which strategies to carry out and stick to them.

- **Prepare**—sell your book at every opportunity.

- **Persistence**—don't give up because you aren't seeing the results of your hard work right away.

➤ **Praise**—give thanks to everyone who helps you.

➤ **Pause**—take time to reflect on your goals and how you're going to achieve them.

➤ **Power**—you have power, now use it.

RESOURCES

Authors need to research before marketing, promoting, and selling their books. In doing so, an author can find many helpful books on the topic. It can overwhelm an author but don't let it stop you from marketing, promoting, and selling your books.

As mentioned before, I found the following books the most helpful.

- 1001 Ways to Market Your Books, John Kremer (Open Horizons 2009)

- Guerrilla Publicity, Jay Conrad Levinson, Rick Frishman, and Jill Lublin (Adams Media Corporation)

- How to Write, Print and Sell Your Book, Dan Poynter (ParaPublishing, 2009)

ABOUT THE AUTHOR

Lorraine M. Harris is a native of Connellsville, Pennsylvania. She retired from the United States government after 34 years. She and her husband, Lamont moved from the Washington, D.C. metropolitan area to The Villages, Florida. They have two daughters, Nicole and Natalie, and a son-in-law, Scott.

As an award-winning author, she conducts workshops and seminars, and teaches courses. She speaks at libraries, book clubs, writing groups and high schools.

Lorraine is a lifetime member of the Florida Writers Association, founder of the Write Corner and member of The Writers League of the Villages.

Since retiring to The Villages, she authored and published numerous fictional books. She has won the National Novel Writing Month (NaNoWriMo) award for three years. In 2008, Lorraine received the honor of Author of the Year by the Artists of America (AOA) in California. AOA provides children in the inner city with opportunities to learn about the arts. In 2011, the African American Golfers Board inducted her in the African American Hall of Fame as the "2011 Golf Publisher of the Year."

Lorraine lives by the saying, *"We make a living by what we get, and we make a life by what we give."* She donates portions of her book sales to a variety of charities.

BOOKS BY LORRAINE

SUNDAY GOLF
AFTER BOWLING
GOLF COURSE VIEW
CASSEROLE PARADE
CASSEROLE SURPRISE
NOT THE NORM, A SMALLTOWN STORY
IT COULD HAPPEN TO YOUR CHILD
BEHIND CLOSED DOORS
LIVING WITH DECEPTION
REGAL CARE
SURVIVING THE LIE
AMY'S ADVENTUROUS BUS TRIP
AMY'S AUTUMN SPLENDOR
INTUITION, CO-AUTHOR, DEBORAH SEIBERT

SELF-HELP BOOKS

MAH JONGG FOR SENIORS, GUARANTEED
MARKETING FOR SELF-PUBLISHED AUTHORS

To obtain additional information about the author, visit her website, www.lorrainemharris. All Lorraine's books are available on Amazon, Barnes and Noble, and other Internet sites selling books.

A NOTE FROM LORRAINE

Thank you for reading, *"Sensible, Successful Book Marketing Tips"* If you found the book helpful, I would love to hear from you. Please take the time and leave a short review on my website, Amazon.com, Twitter, Instagram, or Facebook. It is the nicest compliment I can receive and thank you for doing so.

Please tell your friends. Word of mouth is my best friend and the single most effective way for selling my books.